Five Summer Pieces

ROMANTIC TONE POEMS FOR PIANO SOLO

By Christos Tsitsaros

~ *To Ian Hobson, affectionately* ~

CONTENTS

ISBN 978-1-70512-662-2

Contact us:
Hal Leonard
7777 West Bluemound Road
Milwaukee, WI 53213
Email: info@halleonard.com

In Europe, contact:
Hal Leonard Europe Limited
42 Wigmore Street
Marylebone, London, W1U 2RN
Email: info@halleonardeurope.com

In Australia, contact:
Hal Leonard Australia Pty. Ltd.
4 Lentara Court
Cheltenham, Victoria, 3192 Australia
Email: info@halleonard.com.au

Preface and Performance Notes

The *Five Summer Pieces for Piano Solo* were composed during the summer of 2019 in a spontaneous spur of inspiration. Their evocative character, simultaneous exuberance, optimism, and pianistic flair are all traits that I hope will stir the pianist's imagination and elicit the kinds of emotional responses that I felt while composing them. Driven by an internal poetic narrative, the five pieces form an organic whole characterized by a synthesis of versified stylistic elements and techniques. The dramatic arc evolves from the mysticism of the quasi-impressionistic "Reverie" to the passion and emotional exuberance of "Soaring Exaltation." In contrast, the haunting open harmonies of "Echoes of a Sea Cave" bring in a sense of mystery and wonder. "Evocation" displays internal pathos amidst glimpses of elation and hope. The virtuosic, impassioned "Toccata" drives the series to a powerful and emotionally charged conclusion.

Reverie. The sixteenth notes arpeggiations of the opening section form the canvas upon which the ascending phrases are drawn in different layers; play them lightly, in a melted *legatissimo* touch. At the same time, allow the dramatic dialogue between the voices to unfold naturally, using a warm sound quality and prolonging the underlying harmonies by means of the pedal. In the second theme (mm. 29-51), strive for creating a long perspective through the dynamic and sound color changes at each reiteration of the motive. The ensuing section (mm. 36-61) leads to a climactic reappearance the second theme, soon merging with the material of the first section with renewed energy and passion. Keep the emotional tension throughout the *maestoso* section until the gradual appeasement starting in m. 68. Relish the extemporaneous quality of the final section, giving due emphasis to the *più lento, con lincenza,* rhapsodic statement (mm. 85-86.)

Soaring Exultation. I recommend practicing the long singing phrases of "Soaring Exultation" separately from the thirty-two note accompanying figurations, as well as singing them physically as a means of understanding the inherent *rubato* and the breathing points within them. In contrast, the ensuing section featuring dotted rhythms (mm. 9-14) should be articulated with lightness and rhythmic precision, without losing the support of the underlying harmony through the appropriate use of the pedal, as indicated. Play the accelerando section (mm. 28-33) in the manner of a brilliant cadenza and, following that, simulate orchestral effects by showcasing the shift of the ascending motive between the upper and lower parts of the texture (mm. 35-42). All expressive means (*rubato,* sound, pedal) should converge to render the passion and exuberance of the final restatement of the theme, amidst the different textural transformations. Following this climactic section, let the emotional appeasement of mm. 61 to the end inform your sound and sense of time.

Echoes of a Sea Cave. In "Echoes," the nimble ebb and tide of the waters is suggested by the constant flow of the eighth notes, which should remain more or less even throughout the different meter changes. The tempo should be flexible, fluctuating progressively hand in hand with the dynamic shifts. Make the best out of big, short-range *diminuendos* following sonorous peaks (mm. 15-16, 38-39), and sudden drops of dynamic following long *crescendos* (mm. 18-20, 23-26) to convey the resounding of haunting echoes through the caves. Play the unexpected harmonic shifts with a tender, mysterious color (mm. 10-11, mm. 28-29, 62-63) with optional use of the left pedal. In the development section of the piece (mm. 28-50), can you hear the irresistibly enchanting song of the Sirens, luring Odysseus and his men to shipwreck on the surrounding rocks and cliffs?

Evocation.   A sensitive balance between the melody and the cascading arpeggiated figures is paramount throughout the first section of "Evocation" (mm. 1-14); imagine gliding through the position changes without disturbing the main melodic thread. In the bridge between the first and second themes (mm. 15-25), feel the transition from a melancholy and sober mood to a more luminous and hopeful one through the mode exchange (A major to A minor) and the hemiola rhythmic patterns (mm. 23-25) ushering the uplifting second theme. Keep the underlying accompaniment of this theme (mm. 26-41) light and rhythmically precise, without dragging the tempo. Later, as this motive expands into a more impassioned statement, use *rubato* imaginatively to convey an improvised quality; mm. 65-73 should sound as free as possible. Start the return of the theme (mm. 78 on) as softly and impalpably as possible, before enriching and strengthening the sound amidst the ensuing cascading gestures. Then, withdraw as quickly as possible in mm. 97-98 to make space for the rising dramatic arc of mm. 98-125, in which the material of the bridge is brought to the center spotlight. In the final section of the piece, enjoy the release of dramatic tension by playing it with somewhat distantly, yet with a rich tone and a sense of total freedom.

Toccata.   The dark, ominous color of the *doppio movimento e rigoroso* section of the toccata contrasts with the eerie melody of the opening section. Emphasize this contrast by playing the rapid arpeggiations with a feather-like sound quality, allowing the melody to unfold flexibly and unhurriedly; feel the unsettled, *inquieto* quality of mm. 9-28 by shaping the phrases as indicated, and maintaining a gradual and consistent dynamic and tempo increase leading to the first climactic point in mm. 29-33. This section can be a little faster because of the preceding ascending sweeping chord gestures and the gradual appeasement that follows, leading to the *meno mosso* and *espressivo* section that balances this significant sound and time fluctuation. Here, the melody of the introduction returns emotionally reinvested; express its languishing character with a deep, warm *cantabile* and a flexible tempo. Throughout the ensuing relentless developmental section, it is important to keep the B-flat pedal point resounding in the pedal regardless of the chromatic motion in the upper voices. Play mm. 56-59 with flair, showcasing the contrary motion of the octatonic scales in both hands and leading through sound and time to the second climactic peak in 61-62. Measures 63-72 are in the style of a *cadenza;* I recommend giving them an agitated, precipitous quality. As a word of caution, withdraw the tempo a bit in m. 73, to allow for yet another dramatic surge leading to the boisterous, impetuous section of mm. 78 to the end. In this final section, take advantage of the hemiola rhythmic patterns of mm. 82-83, to add to the virtuoso flair and elated mood of the conclusion.

Special thanks to Charmaine Siagian for undertaking this project and for her invaluable advice and care; and to Kimberly Brand for her many hours of meticulous engraving.

This collection is dedicated to my piano mentor, now colleague, Ian Hobson.

Christos Tsitsaros
April 2021

Reverie

Christos Tsitsaros

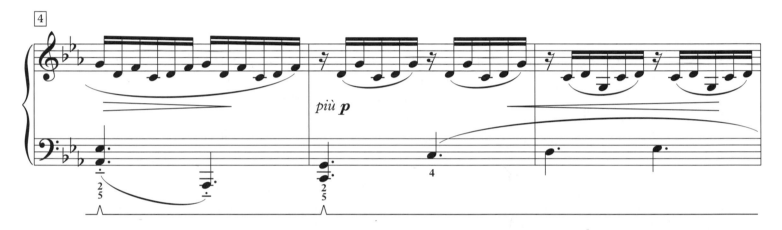

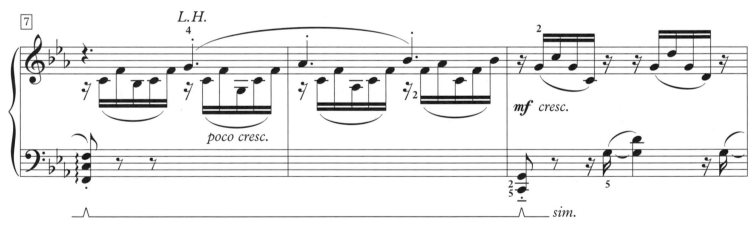

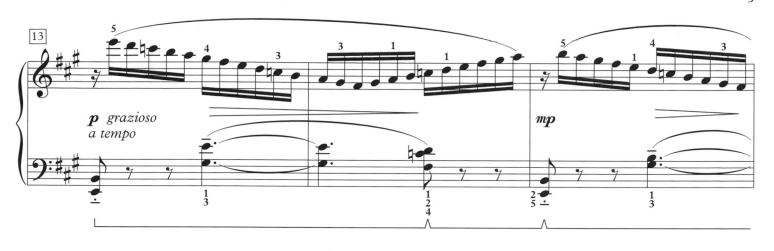

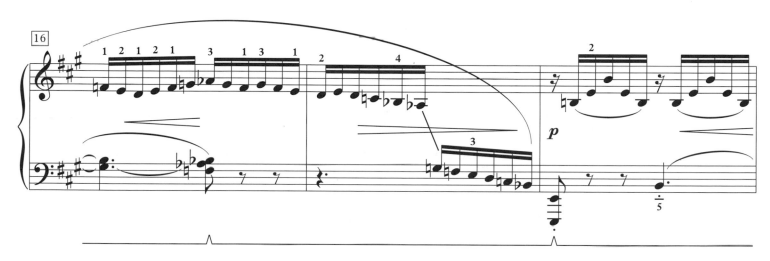

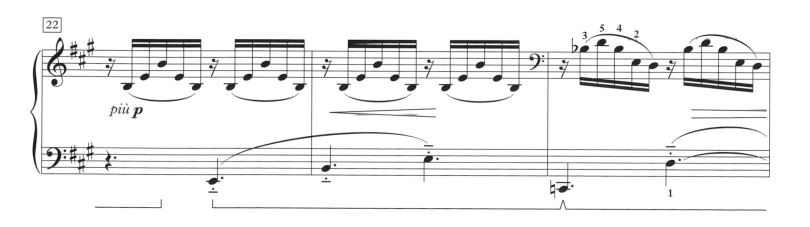

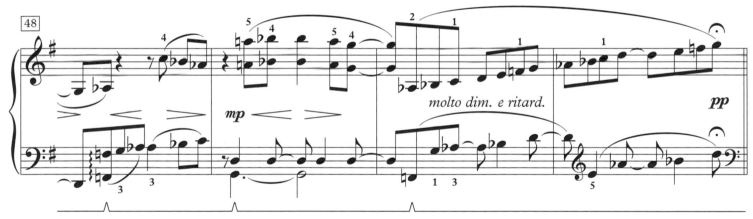

Tempo Primo, maestoso

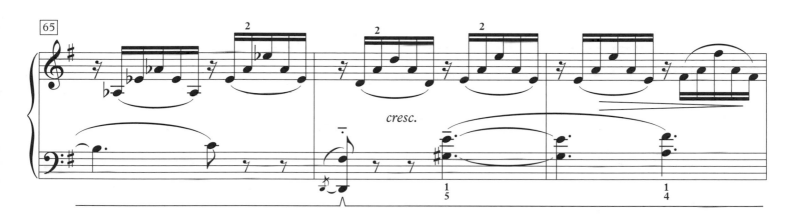

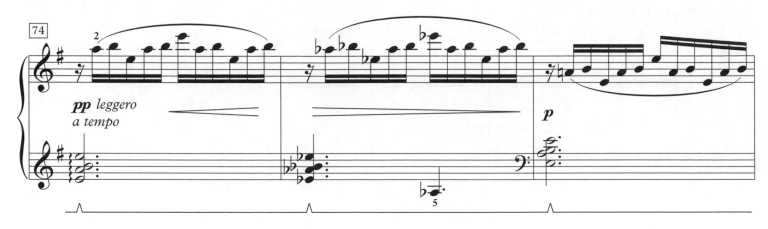

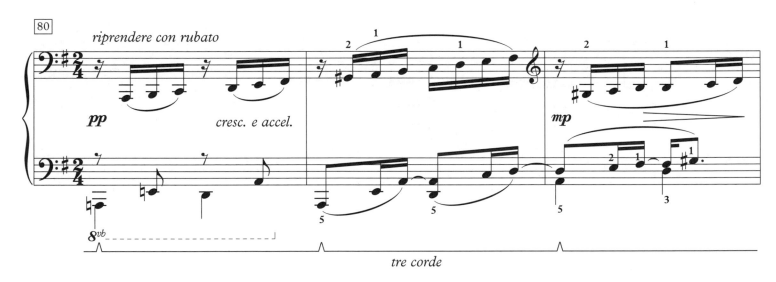

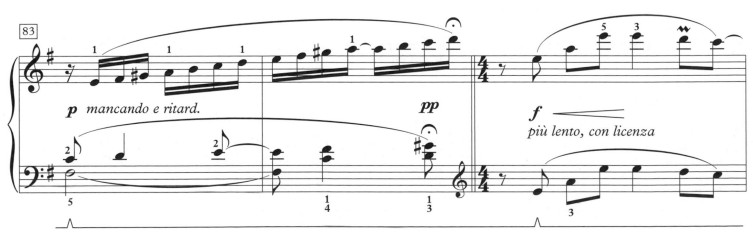

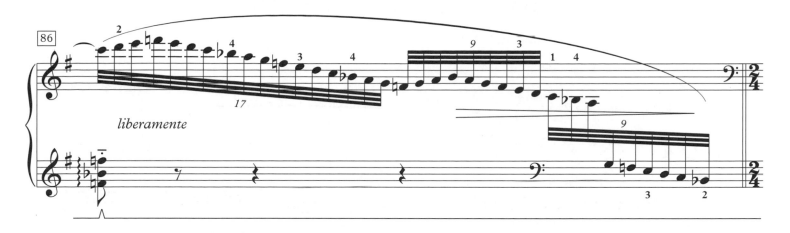

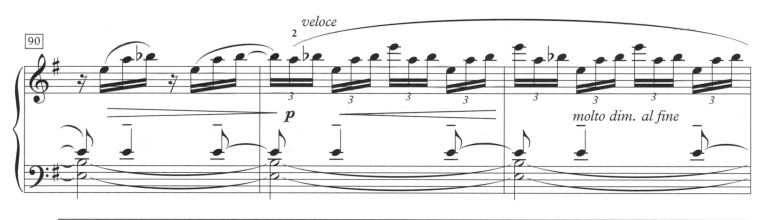

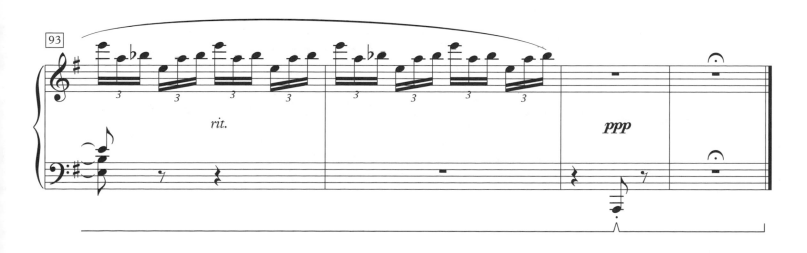

Soaring Exultation

Christos Tsitsaros

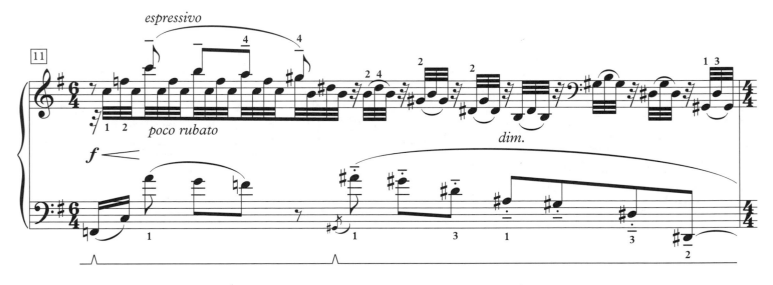

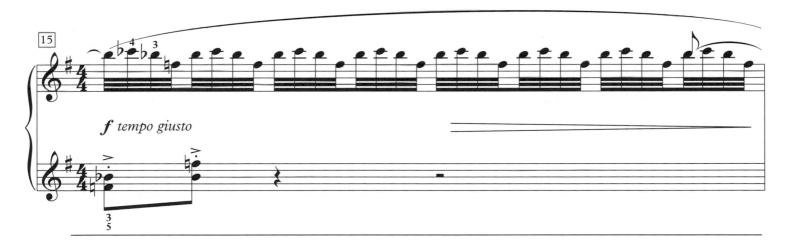

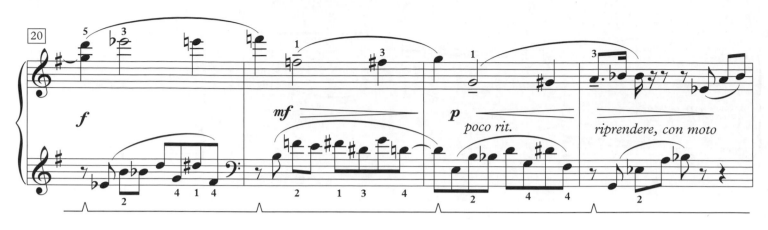

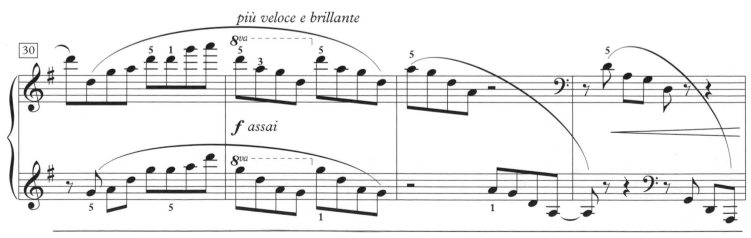

Echoes of a Sea Cave

Christos Tsitsaros

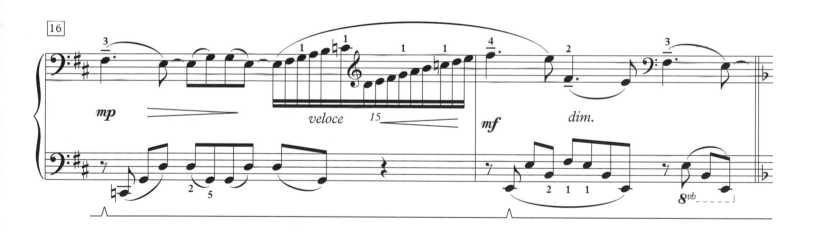

Evocation

Christos Tsitsaros

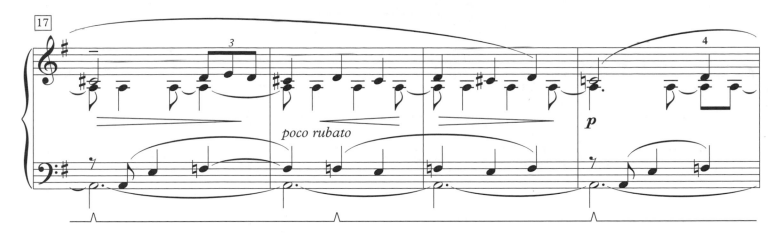

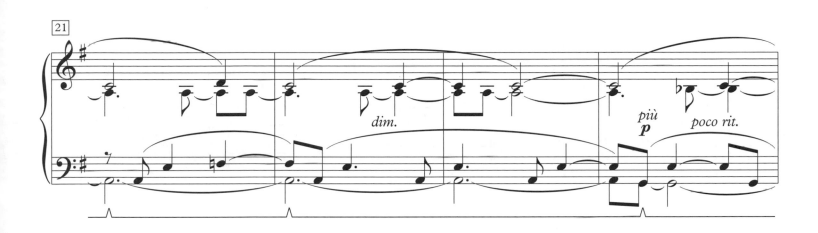

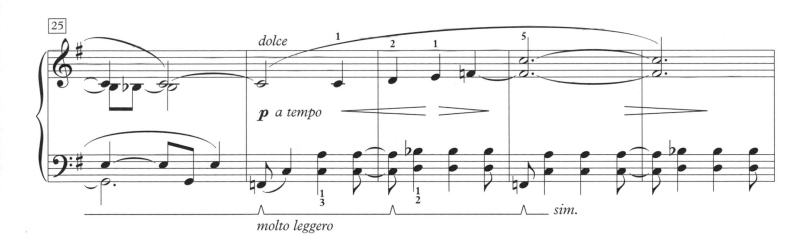

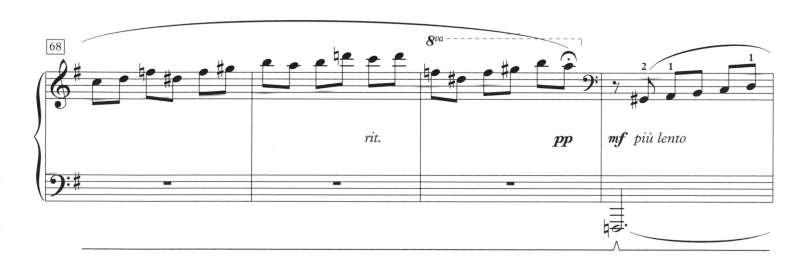

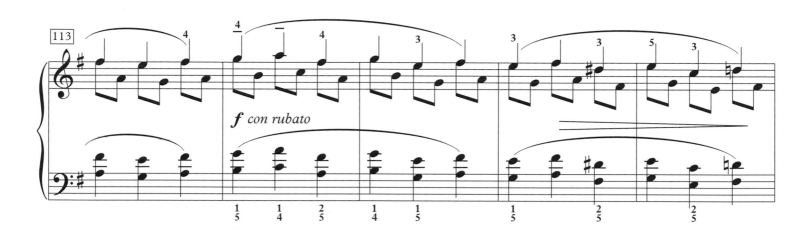

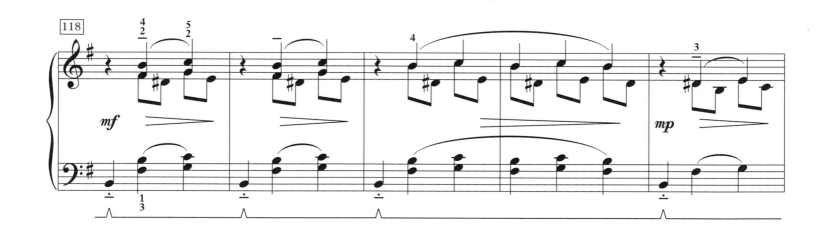

Toccata

Christos Tsitsaros

Allegro moderato

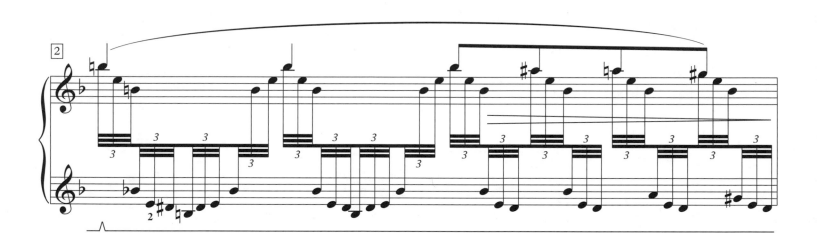

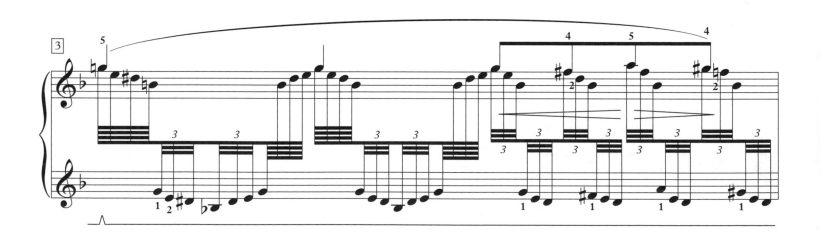

Allegro vivace e rigoroso (doppio movimento)

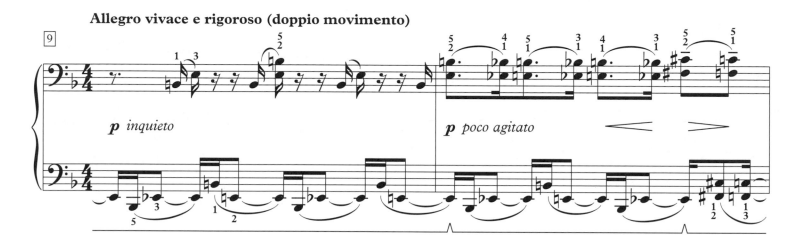

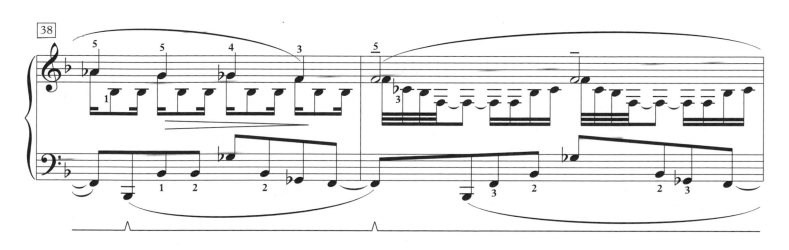

FOLK SONG SERIES

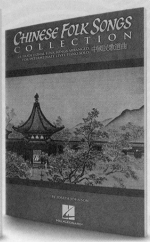

Introduce piano students to the music of world cultures with these folk songs arranged for intermediate piano solo. Each collection features 24 folk songs and includes detailed notes about the folk songs, beautiful illustrations, as well as a map of the regions.

AFRICAN AMERICAN FOLK SONGS COLLECTION

24 TRADITIONAL FOLK SONGS FOR INTERMEDIATE LEVEL PIANO SOLO | *arr. Artina McCain*

The Bamboula • By and By • Deep River • Didn't My Lord Deliver Daniel? • Don't You Let Nobody Turn You Around • Every Time I Feel the Spirit • Give Me That Old Time Religion • Guide My Feet • I Want Jesus to Walk With Me • I Was Way Down A-Yonder • I'm a Soldier, Let Me Ride • In Bright Mansions Above • Lift Ev'ry Voice and Sing • Little David, Play on Your Harp • My Lord, What a Morning • Ride On, King Jesus • Run Mary Run • Sometimes I Feel Like a Motherless Child • Song of Conquest • Take Nabandji • Wade in the Water • Warriors' Song • Watch and Pray • What a Beautiful City.

00358084 Piano Solo.. $10.99

IRISH FOLK SONGS COLLECTION

24 TRADITIONAL FOLK SONGS FOR INTERMEDIATE LEVEL PIANO SOLO | *arr. June Armstrong*

As I Walked Out One Morning • Ballinderry • Blind Mary • Bunclody • Carrickfergus • The Castle of Dromore (The October Winds) • The Cliffs of Doneen • The Coolin • Courtin' in the Kitchen • Down Among the Ditches O • Down by the Salley Gardens • The Fairy Woman of Lough Leane • Follow Me Up to Carlow • The Gartan Mother's Lullaby • Huish the Cat • I'll Tell My Ma • Kitty of Coleraine • The Londonderry Air • My Lagan Love • My Love Is an Arbutus • Rocky Road to Dublin • Slieve Gallion Braes • Squire Parsons • That Night in Bethlehem.

00234359 Piano Solo.. $9.99

MALAY FOLK SONGS COLLECTION

24 TRADITIONAL SONGS ARRANGED FOR INTERMEDIATE LEVEL PIANO SOLO | *arr. Charmaine Siagian*

At Dawn • Chan Mali Chan • C'mon, Mama! • The Cockatoo • The Curvy Water Spinach Stalk • Five Little Chicks • God Bless the Sultan • The Goodbye Song • Great Indonesia • It's All Good Here • The Jumping Frog • Longing • Mak Inang • Milk Coffee • The Moon Kite • Morning Tide • My Country • Onward Singapore • Ponyfish • Song for the Ladybugs • The Stork Song • Suriram • Trek Tek Tek • Voyage of the Sampan.

00288420 Piano Solo.. $10.99

CHINESE FOLK SONGS COLLECTION

24 TRADITIONAL SONGS ARRANGED FOR INTERMEDIATE LEVEL PIANO SOLO | *arr. Joseph Johnson*

Beating the Wild Hog • Blue Flower • Carrying Song • Crescent Moon • Darkening Sky • Digging for Potatoes • Girl's Lament • Great Wall • Hand Drum Song • Homesick • Jasmine Flower Song • Little Cowherd • Love Song of the Prarie • Memorial • Mountaintop View • Northwest Rains • Running Horse Mountain • Sad, Rainy Day • Song of the Clown • The Sun Came Up Happy • Wa-Ha-Ha • Wedding Veil • White Flower • Woven Basket.

00296764 Piano Solo.. $9.99

KOREAN FOLK SONGS COLLECTION

24 TRADITIONAL FOLK SONGS FOR INTERMEDIATE LEVEL PIANO SOLO | arr. Lawrence Lee

Arirang • Autumn in the City • Birdie, Birdie • Boat Song • Catch the Tail • Chestnut • Cricket • Dance in the Moonlight • Five Hundred Years • Flowers • Fun Is Here • The Gate • Han River • Harvest • Jindo Field Song • Lullaby • The Mill • The Palace • The Pier • Three-Way Junction • Waterfall • Wild Herbs • Yearning • You and I.

00296810 Piano Solo.. $9.99

JAPANESE FOLK SONGS COLLECTION

24 TRADITIONAL FOLK SONGS FOR INTERMEDIATE LEVEL PIANO SOLO | *arr. Mika Goto*

Blooming Flowers • Come Here, Fireflies • Counting Game • The Fisherman's Song • Going to the Shrine • Harvest Song • Itsuki Lullaby • Joyful Doll Festival • Kimigayo • Let's Sing • My Hometown • Picking Tea Leaves • The Rabbit on the Moon • Rain • Rain Showers • Rock-Paper-Scissors • Sakura • Seven Baby Crows • Takeda Lullaby • Time to Go Home • Village Festival • Where Are You From? • Wish I Could Go • You're It!

00296891 Piano Solo.. $9.99

halleonard.com

Prices, contents and availability subject to change without notice.

POPULAR SONGS
HAL LEONARD STUDENT PIANO LIBRARY

The **Hal Leonard Student Piano Library** has great songs, and you will find all your favorites here: Disney classics, Broadway and movie favorites, and today's top hits. These graded collections are skillfully and imaginatively arranged for students and pianists at every level, from elementary solos with teacher accompaniments to sophisticated piano solos for the advancing pianist.

Adele
arr. Mona Rejino
Correlates with HLSPL Level 5
00159590...............................$12.99

The Beatles
arr. Eugénie Rocherolle
Correlates with HLSPL Level 5
00296649................................ $12.99

Irving Berlin Piano Duos
arr. Don Heitler and Jim Lyke
Correlates with HLSPL Level 5
00296838.............................$14.99

Broadway Favorites
arr. Phillip Keveren
Correlates with HLSPL Level 4
00279192.............................$12.99

Chart Hits
arr. Mona Rejino
Correlates with HLSPL Level 5
00296710..............................$8.99

Christmas at the Piano
arr. Lynda Lybeck-Robinson
Correlates with HLSPL Level 4
00298194.............................$12.99

Christmas Cheer
arr. Phillip Keveren
Correlates with HLSPL Level 4
00296616..............................$8.99

Classic Christmas Favorites
arr. Jennifer & Mike Watts
Correlates with HLSPL Level 5
00129582.............................$9.99

Christmas Time Is Here
arr. Eugénie Rocherolle
Correlates with HLSPL Level 5
00296614..............................$8.99

Classic Joplin Rags
arr. Fred Kern
Correlates with HLSPL Level 5
00296743.............................$9.99

Classical Pop – Lady Gaga Fugue & Other Pop Hits
arr. Giovanni Dettori
Correlates with HLSPL Level 5
00296921.............................$12.99

Contemporary Movie Hits
arr. by Carol Klose, Jennifer Linn and Wendy Stevens
Correlates with HLSPL Level 5
00296780................................$8.99

Contemporary Pop Hits
arr. Wendy Stevens
Correlates with HLSPL Level 3
00296836...............................$8.99

Cool Pop
arr. Mona Rejino
Correlates with HLSPL Level 5
00360103..............................$12.99

Country Favorites
arr. Mona Rejino
Correlates with HLSPL Level 5
00296861................................$9.99

Disney Favorites
arr. Phillip Keveren
Correlates with HLSPL Levels 3/4
00296647...........................$10.99

Disney Film Favorites
arr. Mona Rejino
Correlates with HLSPL Level 5
00296809 ....$10.99

Disney Piano Duets
arr. Jennifer & Mike Watts
Correlates with HLSPL Level 5
00113759..............................$13.99

Double Agent! Piano Duets
arr. Jeremy Siskind
Correlates wlth HLSPL Level 5
00121595..............................$12.99

Easy Christmas Duets
arr. Mona Rejino & Phillip Keveren
Correlates with HLSPL Levels 3/4
00237139.............................$9.99

Easy Disney Duets
arr. Jennifer and Mike Watts
Correlates with HLSPL Level 4
00243727.............................$12.99

Four Hands on Broadway
arr. Fred Kern
Correlates with HLSPL Level 5
00146177.............................$12.99

Frozen Piano Duets
arr. Mona Rejino
Correlates with HLSPL Levels 3/4
00144294..............................$12.99

Hip-Hop for Piano Solo
arr. Logan Evan Thomas
Correlates with HLSPL Level 5
00360950..............................$12.99

Jazz Hits for Piano Duet
arr. Jeremy Siskind
Correlates with HLSPL Level 5
00143248..........................$12.99

Elton John
arr. Carol Klose
Correlates with HLSPL Level 5
00296721..............................$10.99

Joplin Ragtime Duets
arr. Fred Kern
Correlates with HLSPL Level 5
00296771................................$8.99

Movie Blockbusters
arr. Mona Rejino
Correlates with HLSPL Level 5
00232850..............................$10.99

The Nutcracker Suite
arr. Lynda Lybeck-Robinson
Correlates with HLSPL Levels 3/4
00147906...............................$8.99

Pop Hits for Piano Duet
arr. Jeremy Siskind
Correlates with HLSPL Level 5
00224734............................$12.99

Sing to the King
arr. Phillip Keveren
Correlates with HLSPL Level 5
00296808...............................$8.99

Smash Hits
arr. Mona Rejino
Correlates with HLSPL Level 5
00284841.............................$10.99

Spooky Halloween Tunes
arr. Fred Kern
Correlates with HLSPL Levels 3/4
00121550...............................$9.99

Today's Hits
arr. Mona Rejino
Correlates with HLSPL Level 5
00296646..............................$9.99

Top Hits
arr. Jennifer and Mike Watts
Correlates with HLSPL Level 5
00296894............................$10.99

Top Piano Ballads
arr. Jennifer Watts
Correlates with HLSPL Level 5
00197926.............................$10.99

Video Game Hits
arr. Mona Rejino
Correlates with HLSPL Level 4
00300310.,,,,,,,,,,,,,,,,,,,,,,,,,$12.99

You Raise Me Up
arr. Deborah Brady
Correlates with HLSPL Level 2/3
00296576..............................$7.95

COMPOSER SHOWCASE
HAL LEONARD STUDENT PIANO LIBRARY

This series showcases great original piano music from our **Hal Leonard Student Piano Library** family of composers. Carefully graded for easy selection.

BILL BOYD

JAZZ BITS (AND PIECES)
Early Intermediate Level
00290312 11 Solos......................$7.99

JAZZ DELIGHTS
Intermediate Level
00240435 11 Solos......................$8.99

JAZZ FEST
Intermediate Level
00240436 10 Solos......................$8.99

JAZZ PRELIMS
Early Elementary Level
00290032 12 Solos......................$7.99

JAZZ SKETCHES
Intermediate Level
00220001 8 Solos........................$8.99

JAZZ STARTERS
Elementary Level
00290425 10 Solos......................$8.99

JAZZ STARTERS II
Late Elementary Level
00290434 11 Solos......................$7.99

JAZZ STARTERS III
Late Elementary Level
00290465 12 Solos......................$8.99

THINK JAZZ!
Early Intermediate Level
00290417 Method Book............$12.99

TONY CARAMIA

JAZZ MOODS
Intermediate Level
00296728 8 Solos........................$6.95

SUITE DREAMS
Intermediate Level
00296775 4 Solos........................$6.99

SONDRA CLARK

DAKOTA DAYS
Intermediate Level
00296521 5 Solos........................$6.95

FLORIDA FANTASY SUITE
Intermediate Level
00296766 3 Duets.......................$7.95

THREE ODD METERS
Intermediate Level
00296472 3 Duets.......................$6.95

MATTHEW EDWARDS

CONCERTO FOR YOUNG PIANISTS
FOR 2 PIANOS, FOUR HANDS
Intermediate Level Book/CD
00296356 3 Movements $19.99

CONCERTO NO. 2 IN G MAJOR
FOR 2 PIANOS, 4 HANDS
Intermediate Level Book/CD
00296670 3 Movements............$17.99

PHILLIP KEVEREN

MOUSE ON A MIRROR
Late Elementary Level
00296361 5 Solos........................$8.99

MUSICAL MOODS
Elementary/Late Elementary Level
00296714 7 Solos........................$6.99

SHIFTY-EYED BLUES
Late Elementary Level
00296374 5 Solos........................$7.99

CAROL KLOSE

THE BEST OF CAROL KLOSE
Early to Late Intermediate Level
00146151 15 Solos....................$12.99

CORAL REEF SUITE
Late Elementary Level
00296354 7 Solos........................$7.50

DESERT SUITE
Intermediate Level
00296667 6 Solos........................$7.99

FANCIFUL WALTZES
Early Intermediate Level
00296473 5 Solos........................$7.95

GARDEN TREASURES
Late Intermediate Level
00296787 5 Solos........................$8.50

ROMANTIC EXPRESSIONS
Intermediate to Late Intermediate Level
00296923 5 Solos........................$8.99

WATERCOLOR MINIATURES
Early Intermediate Level
00296848 7 Solos........................$7.99

JENNIFER LINN

AMERICAN IMPRESSIONS
Intermediate Level
00296471 6 Solos........................$8.99

ANIMALS HAVE FEELINGS TOO
Early Elementary/Elementary Level
00147789 8 Solos........................$8.99

AU CHOCOLAT
Late Elementary/Early Intermediate Level
00298110 7 Solos........................$8.99

CHRISTMAS IMPRESSIONS
Intermediate Level
00296706 8 Solos........................$8.99

JUST PINK
Elementary Level
00296722 9 Solos........................$8.99

LES PETITES IMAGES
Late Elementary Level
00296664 7 Solos........................$8.99

LES PETITES IMPRESSIONS
Intermediate Level
00296355 6 Solos........................$8.99

REFLECTIONS
Late Intermediate Level
00296843 5 Solos........................$8.99

TALES OF MYSTERY
Intermediate Level
00296769 6 Solos........................$8.99

LYNDA LYBECK-ROBINSON

ALASKA SKETCHES
Early Intermediate Level
00119637 8 Solos........................$8.99

AN AWESOME ADVENTURE
Late Elementary Level
00137563 8 Solos........................$7.99

FOR THE BIRDS
Early Intermediate/Intermediate Level
00237078 9 Solos........................$8.99

WHISPERING WOODS
Late Elementary Level
00275905 9 Solos........................$8.99

MONA REJINO

CIRCUS SUITE
Late Elementary Level
00296665 5 Solos........................$8.99

COLOR WHEEL
Early Intermediate Level
00201951 6 Solos........................$9.99

IMPRESIONES DE ESPAÑA
Intermediate Level
00337520 6 Solos........................$8.99

IMPRESSIONS OF NEW YORK
Intermediate Level
00364212.................................$8.99

JUST FOR KIDS
Elementary Level
00296840 8 Solos........................$7.99

MERRY CHRISTMAS MEDLEYS
Intermediate Level
00296799 5 Solos........................$8.99

MINIATURES IN STYLE
Intermediate Level
00148088 6 Solos........................$8.99

PORTRAITS IN STYLE
Early Intermediate Level
00296507 6 Solos........................$8.99

EUGÉNIE ROCHEROLLE

CELEBRATION SUITE
Intermediate Level
00152724 3 Duets.......................$8.99

ENCANTOS ESPAÑOLES (SPANISH DELIGHTS)
Intermediate Level
00125451 6 Solos........................$8.99

JAMBALAYA
Intermediate Level
00296654 2 Pianos, 8 Hands.....$12.99
00296725 2 Pianos, 4 Hands.......$7.95

JEROME KERN CLASSICS
Intermediate Level
00296577 10 Solos....................$12.99

LITTLE BLUES CONCERTO
Early Intermediate Level
00142801 2 Pianos, 4 Hands......$12.99

TOUR FOR TWO
Late Elementary Level
00296832 6 Duets.......................$9.99

TREASURES
Late Elementary/Early Intermediate Level
00296924 7 Solos........................$8.99

JEREMY SISKIND

BIG APPLE JAZZ
Intermediate Level
00278209 8 Solos........................$8.99

MYTHS AND MONSTERS
Late Elementary/Early Intermediate Level
00148148 9 Solos........................$8.99

CHRISTOS TSITSAROS

DANCES FROM AROUND THE WORLD
Early Intermediate Level
00296688 7 Solos........................$8.99

FIVE SUMMER PIECES
Late Intermediate/Advanced Level
00361235 5 Solos......................$12.99

LYRIC BALLADS
Intermediate/Late Intermediate Level
00102404 6 Solos........................$8.99

POETIC MOMENTS
Intermediate Level
00296403 8 Solos........................$8.99

SEA DIARY
Early Intermediate Level
00253486 9 Solos........................$8.99

SONATINA HUMORESQUE
Late Intermediate Level
00296772 3 Movements.............$6.99

SONGS WITHOUT WORDS
Intermediate Level
00296506 9 Solos........................$9.99

THREE PRELUDES
Early Advanced Level
00130747 3 Solos........................$8.99

THROUGHOUT THE YEAR
Late Elementary Level
00296723 12 Duets....................$6.95

ADDITIONAL COLLECTIONS

AT THE LAKE
by Elvina Pearce
Elementary/Late Elementary Level
00131642 10 Solos and Duets.....$7.99

CHRISTMAS FOR TWO
by Dan Fox
Early Intermediate Level
00290069 13 Duets....................$8.99

CHRISTMAS JAZZ
by Mike Springer
Intermediate Level
00296525 6 Solos........................$8.99

COUNTY RAGTIME FESTIVAL
by Fred Kern
Intermediate Level
00296882 7 Solos........................$7.99

LITTLE JAZZERS
by Jennifer Watts
Elementary/Late Elementary Level
00154573 9 Solos........................$8.99

PLAY THE BLUES!
by Luann Carman
Early Intermediate Level
00296357 10 Solos.....................$9.99

ROLLER COASTERS & RIDES
by Jennifer & Mike Watts
Intermediate Level
00131144 8 Duets.......................$8.99

www.halleonard.com

Prices, contents, and availability subject to change without notice.